First published 2012 by Modern Toss Ltd.
Modern Toss, PO Box 386, Brighton BN1 3SN, England
www.moderntoss.com

ISBN 978-0-9564191-2-5

Desperate Business first appeared in Private Eye

A CIP catalogue record for this book is available from the British Library.

Designed and typeset by Modern Toss
Printed and bound by Proost Belgium

Visit www.moderntoss.com to read more about all our books and to buy them yeah.
You will also find lots of other shit there, and you can sign up to our mailing list so
that you're always kept bang up to date with it, cheers.

MODERN TOSS PRESENTS

by Jon Link and Mick Bunnage

DESPERATE BUSINESS

Hello I was just in the area and wondered if
I could interest you in a pole dance?

DESPERATE BUSINESS

DESPERATE BUSINESS

DESPERATE BUSINESS

DESPERATE BUSINESS

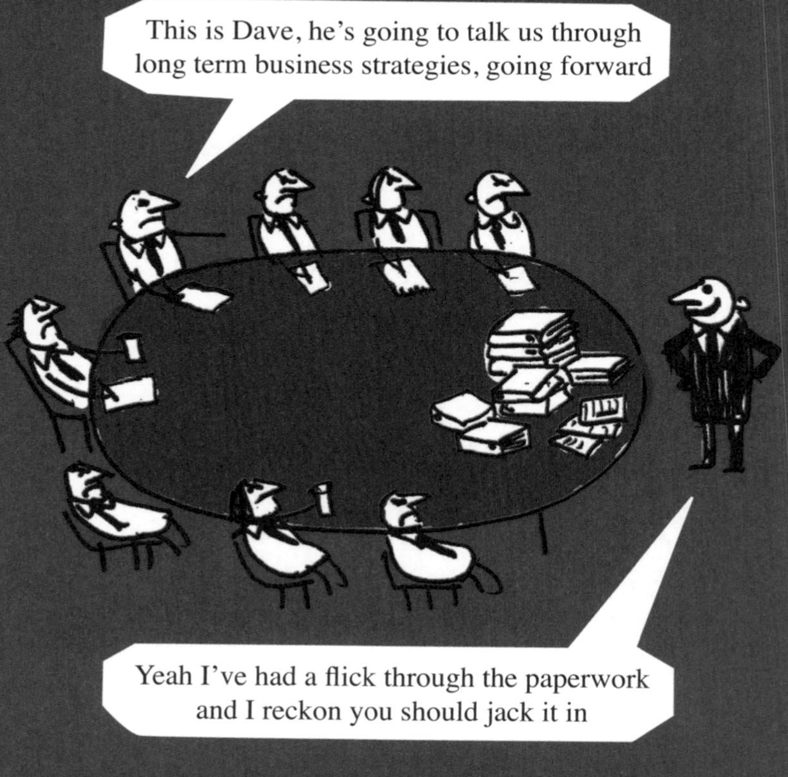

DESPERATE BUSINESS

DESPERATE BUSINESS

DESPERATE BUSINESS

DESPERATE BUSINESS

DESPERATE BUSINESS

DESPERATE BUSINESS

DESPERATE BUSINESS

DESPERATE BUSINESS

DESPERATE BUSINESS

DESPERATE BUSINESS

DESPERATE BUSINESS

DESPERATE BUSINESS

DESPERATE BUSINESS

DESPERATE BUSINESS

DESPERATE BUSINESS

DESPERATE BUSINESS

DESPERATE BUSINESS

We've decided to have a bit of fun with the old holiday thing this year. First person to ask for one gets the sack.

DESPERATE BUSINESS

DESPERATE BUSINESS

DESPERATE BUSINESS

DESPERATE BUSINESS

DESPERATE BUSINESS

Alright mate, do you want to buy some paparazzi style portraits of your family? That's your wife topless in the back garden

DESPERATE BUSINESS

DESPERATE BUSINESS

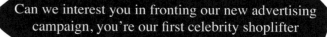

DESPERATE BUSINESS

DESPERATE BUSINESS

DESPERATE BUSINESS

We're exploring new business opportunities.
Carry on with the accounts but every time
that red light comes on slip your top off

DESPERATE BUSINESS

Yeah in the long run having him put down is the cheapest option, but he does only need worming

DESPERATE BUSINESS

DESPERATE BUSINESS

DESPERATE BUSINESS

DESPERATE BUSINESS

DESPERATE BUSINESS

DESPERATE BUSINESS

DESPERATE BUSINESS

Martin's just invited us over for dinner, he says can we bring a bottle and something to eat

DESPERATE BUSINESS

DESPERATE BUSINESS

DESPERATE BUSINESS

DESPERATE BUSINESS

DESPERATE BUSINESS

DESPERATE BUSINESS

DESPERATE BUSINESS